Max's book of The village of Dent

Contents

Nelson

Where is Dent?

Hello! My name is Rose.

I live in Dent.

Dent is a **village** in
the north
of England.

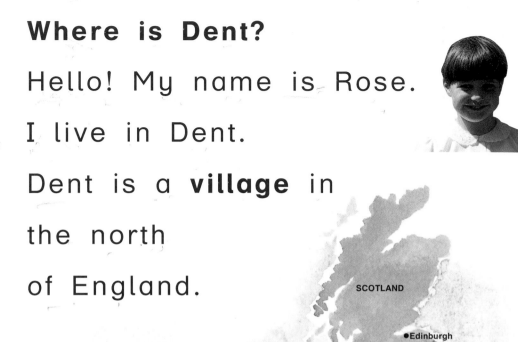

Can you see Dent on this map?

This is a map of Dent.

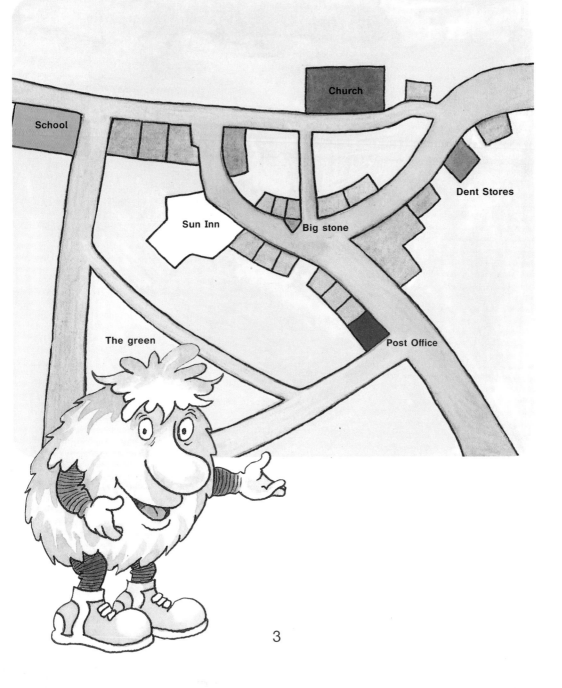

School

Church

Dent Stores

Sun Inn

Big stone

The green

Post Office

3

Our farm

I live on a farm.

This is my house.

Is your house

like this?

We keep sheep on our farm.

Dad **shears** the sheep.

The wool from
the sheep is
made into clothes.

My jumper is
made of wool.

Max Fact

Long ago, the people
in Dent made lots of
clothes from wool.
They were called the
Knitters of Dent.

The village

The shop

The shop is called Dent Stores.

We buy food here.

What else can you buy in
Dent Stores?

The church

The church is near the shop.

The clock tells the time.

When it **chimes** you can

hear it all over Dent.

The big stone

Can you see the big stone?

It is in the middle of Dent.

There is a fountain in it.

The Sun Inn

The Sun Inn is very old.

Max Fact

Long ago, there were no cars.

People rode horses.

The steps helped people

get on the horses.

9

The Post Office

This is the Post Office.

We buy stamps and

postcards here.

We buy ice cream here too!

The green

We play on the green after school.

Can you see what we play on?

I like the slide best!

My school

My school is very small.

There are only two classes.

This is my class.

This is my teacher.

How many classes are there in YOUR school?

This is where we eat our dinner.

Each week the old people of

Dent come to school.

They eat dinner with us.

Quiz

Look at the map on page 3.

Can you see...

the Sun Inn?

the big stone?

the green?

the Post Office?

the church?

Glossary

A glossary tells us what

hard words mean.

When a clock **chimes** it makes a sound

    like a bell.

When Dad **shears** the sheep he cuts

    off the wool.

A **village** is like a town but it is

    much smaller.

Index